MOMMYHOOD
— AT ITS —
FINEST

A JOURNEY OF LOVE, LEARNING, AND GROWTH

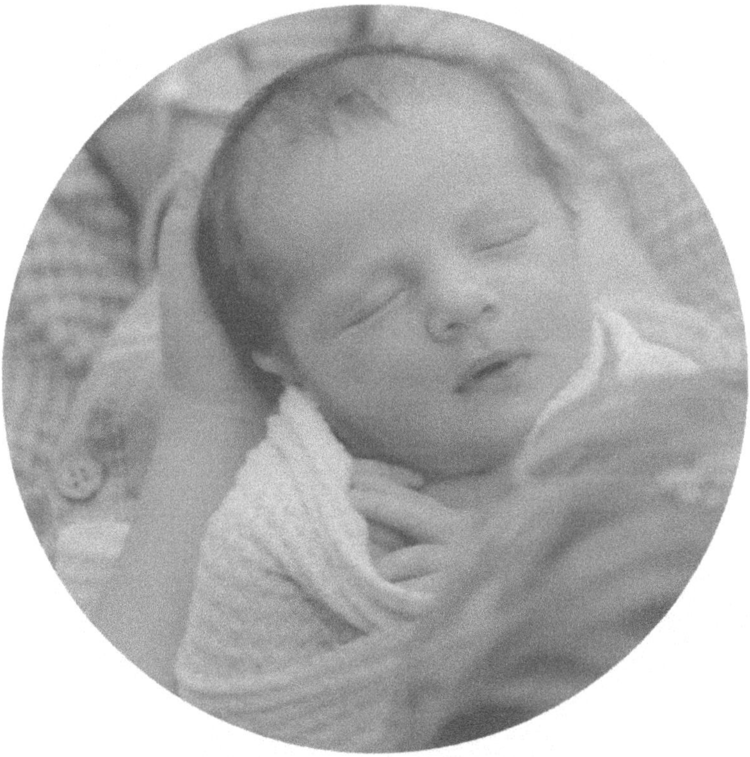

ALEXIS RENEE

TABLE OF CONTENTS

Preface: Embracing the Beauty of Mommyhood 5

Introduction: Celebrating the Journey of Motherhood 7

Part One: Pregnancy and Birth **9**

Two Lines 10

Mom Norms 11

God's Blessing 12

Mother's Loving Womb 13

A Mother's Heart 14

Unborn Child 15

Flutter 16

Tick Tock Time pt. I 17

Contraction 18

The Cord 19

Cutting the Chord 20

Postpartum 21

Forever & Always 22

A Mother's Smile 23

The Unconditional Love of a Mother 24

Loss of a Child 25

Fears 26

Rainbow Baby 27

Part Two: Postpartum and Newborn Breastfeeding **29**

A Mother's Love 30

The Small Battlefield 31

Should I Sleep, Eat, Or…? 32

Fragile Resilience 33

Milk 34

Liquid Gold 35

Public Stare Down 36

The Magic of a Mother's Touch 37

Unbreakable Bond.................................38

A Mother's Voice 39

Baby Teething.................................40

Me and I 41

Sleepless Nights 42

Droopy Eyes.................................44

Boobies, Where Did You Go?.................................45

The Symbol of Producing 46

A Mother's Hug.................................47

Part Three: Watching Them Grow — Through the Good, Bad, and Ugly **49**

To-Do 50

Tick Tock Time pt. II 52

A Mother's Wisdom 53

Chaos.................................54

Mom(ents) pt. I.................................56

Hot Shower.................................57

Step Moms 58

Breaking Habits.................................59

No Time to Pass Me By 60

Laundry, Endless Laundry 61

Overstimulated 62

Mom(ents) pt. II 63

Handbook.................................64

The Strength of a Mother 65

The Future of Tomorrow 66

To My Mom 67

The Dance of Motherhood 68

A Mother's Legacy 69

A Mother's Sacrifice.................................70

Dial Tone.................................71

Acknowledgments.................................72

EMBRACING THE BEAUTY
OF MOMMYHOOD

I am overjoyed to share with you this heartfelt collection of poems titled "Mommyhood at Its Finest." As a mother myself, I have embarked on a journey filled with love, growth, and countless precious moments. It is through this journey that I have discovered the immense beauty and power of motherhood.

When I first became a mother, I was filled with a mix of excitement and apprehension. I knew that this new chapter of my life would bring challenges, but I was also eager to experience the unconditional love and joy that comes with raising a child. Little did I know just how transformative and rewarding this journey would be.

As I navigated the ups and downs of motherhood, I found solace and inspiration in writing. It became my sanctuary, a space where I could pour out my emotions, reflect on my experiences, and celebrate the incredible bond between a mother and her child. It was through these poems that I discovered the power of words to capture the essence of motherhood.

I wrote this book as a tribute to all the mothers out there who tirelessly give their all to their children. It is a celebration of the strength, resilience, and unwavering love that mothers embody. Through these poems, I hope to honor the beauty of the everyday moments, the sacrifices made, and the profound impact that mothers have on their children's lives.

In "Mommyhood at Its Finest," you will find poems that explore the joys of cuddles and laughter, the challenges of sleepless nights and tantrums, and the bittersweet moments of watching our children grow. These poems are a reflection of the raw and authentic experiences that make up the tapestry of motherhood.

I wrote this book not only to share my own journey but also to create a space for mothers to feel seen, heard, and understood. Motherhood can be both incredibly rewarding and incredibly challenging, and it is important to acknowledge and honor the full spectrum of emotions that come with it.

I invite you, dear readers, to join me on this journey of motherhood. Whether you are a mother yourself, have a mother, or simply appreciate the beauty of this role, I hope that these poems will resonate with you. May they serve as a reminder that you are not alone in your experiences and that the love and dedication you pour into your children is truly remarkable.

Thank you for allowing me to share my heart and soul with you through these poems. It is my hope that they will bring comfort, inspiration, and a sense of connection to all those who read them. May they serve as a reminder of the incredible power and love that exists within the bond between a mother and her child.

INTRODUCTION

CELEBRATING THE JOURNEY OF MOTHERHOOD

I am thrilled to present to you this heartfelt collection of poems titled "Mommyhood at Its Finest." This book is a celebration of the extraordinary journey of motherhood, filled with love, joy, challenges, and growth. It is a tribute to all the incredible mothers out there who pour their hearts and souls into raising their children with unwavering dedication and unconditional love.

Motherhood is a transformative experience that shapes us in ways we never thought possible. It is a journey that takes us through the highs and lows, the laughter and tears, and the moments of pure bliss and exhaustion. It is a journey that tests our patience, resilience, and capacity for love.

In this collection of poems, I have sought to capture the essence of motherhood in all its beauty and complexity. Each poem is a reflection of the unique experiences, emotions, and moments that make up the tapestry of motherhood. From the tender moments of bonding and nurturing to the challenges of balancing responsibilities and self-care, these poems aim to resonate with mothers from all walks of life.

Through the power of words, I hope to convey the depth of love, sacrifice, and joy that comes with being a mother. These poems are a testament to the strength and resilience of mothers, who often put their own needs aside to prioritize the well-being and happiness of their children. They are a reminder that motherhood is not always glamorous or easy, but it is a journey filled with immeasurable rewards and blessings.

I invite you, dear readers, to embark on this journey with me. Whether you are a mother yourself, have a mother, or simply appreciate the beauty of motherhood, I hope that these poems will touch your heart and resonate with your own experiences. May they serve as a reminder of the incredible power and love that exists within the bond between a mother and her child.

I am deeply grateful for the opportunity to share these poems with you. It is my hope that they will bring comfort, inspiration, and a sense of connection to all those who read them. May they serve as a tribute to the extraordinary mothers who shape our lives and leave an indelible mark on our hearts.

With love and admiration.

PART ONE:

PREGNANCY AND BIRTH

TWO LINES

This is normal.

It's supposed to shock me.

Which is normal, right?

Every new mother

should relate to this first time.

I'm not overreacting.

But why is there a voice

in my head

telling me,

"Are you sure it's nothing serious?"

And so, I tested it out.

Lo and behold,

there were two visible lines.

Oh, how happy I am to see those signs!

MOM NORMS

This is perfectly normal.

Something about the belly —

Growing like a balloon,

Kicking as if a horse,

And eating like there's no tomorrow.

What's inside?

What could there be

but not a living organism?

Could you take a guess?

GOD'S BLESSING

It will forever fascinate me

On how a woman's body works.

The insides adjust and readjust;

All this is to cater to growing cells

and into the likes of you and me.

I used to pray for things like:

the cold gel rubbed on my belly,

the kicking sensation,

and figuring out what name to give.

Every night for the next nine months,

Until the day comes when this little one is due,

I'll continue to put my hands together

thus, say my innermost wish in hopes

of being fulfilled by the One who listens.

MOTHER'S LOVING WOMB

13

The womb of the mother.

Love,

Sacrifice,

Joy,

Calmness,

Hope.

Bringing hope for peace in the world.

Bulging belly extending

Like God's hand,

Shoving,

Stretching,

Scars,

Showing us all the miracles of life.

A MOTHER'S HEART

14

A heart so full, a love so deep,

A mother's heart, a treasure to keep.

Through thick and thin, she'll always be,

A guiding light, for eternity.

UNBORN CHILD

15

To my unborn baby.

Looking at the video screen,

wandering into space.

"What will you be?"

Thinking will your hair be red or brown?

See you sucking your fingers —

it is truly mesmerizing.

Brown, blue, or green eyes.

Who knows?

As long as you're a healthy beautiful baby.

Boy or girl,

it doesn't matter.

Oh, that heartbeat.

FLUTTER

Oh, that first flutter —

The tiny movement of your kick.

Oh, those moments I'll surely miss.

As you kick your foot in my rib.

I touch it —

you kick again.

Oh, these moments I miss.

TICK TOCK TIME PT. I

17

Tick-tock as the time runs.

Those two hands stranded inside,

Pointing at each number

From one to twelve.

How I wish they'd slow down

and how I hope for the moments

to take their sweet, lovely time

happening and becoming memories.

CONTRACTION

From the first contraction,

piercing pain —

There's medicine given.

Hunched over — too bouncy on a ball.

Wanting the pain to subside.

Medicine dripped in my veins —

the contractions coming in closer and closer.

"Push!"

They spoke.

1, 2, 3.

Breathe in –

Breathe out –

I see his head.

There's the adrenaline rush.

Handed to me,

but I'm so exhausted.

Time to feed and hold him close.

Oh, the first kiss.

THE CORD

You and I are connected.

That cord that has been attached

for quite some time.

This cord has done its work,

right from the start.

Giving you nourishment

and bringing us together as one.

With a strength of a lion,

It has withstood any test.

You and I are connected.

CUTTING THE CHORD

Looking around,

there's a precious smile on his face,

as he cuts the cord.

POSTPARTUM

there is a stillness that floods

at that moment,

the cutting chord moment,

it resounds between these four corners.

~

a stillness

that is simultaneously

happy, exhausted, sad, lost,

all immediately,

at once.

~

depression and joy,

a one-two punch of

tranquility floods

right at that moment.

~

the shock appears,

the glimpse of relief,

of joy shining,

a slow jolt coming through.

FOREVER & ALWAYS

22

I am in love with those little hands.

I am in love with those tiny feet.

I am in love with the chuckles and laughs.

All these I will always look forward to.

In the next years to come,

no matter how tall and big they get,

they will always be my little ones

forever and always.

A MOTHER'S SMILE

23

Her smile, a ray of sunshine bright,

Bringing warmth and joy, day and night.

With every smile, she lights the way,

A mother's love, forever on display.

THE UNCONDITIONAL LOVE OF A MOTHER

In the darkest of nights, a light shines bright,

A mother's love, a beacon of light.

It knows no boundaries, it knows no end,

A love that's unconditional, a love that won't bend.

Through thick and thin, through joy and strife,

A mother's love is a constant in life.

She loves them when they're happy, when they're sad,

She loves them when they're good, when they're bad.

Her love is a shelter, a safe haven,

A place where they find solace, where they're forgiven.

A mother's love, a gift from above,

A love that's eternal, a love that's pure love.

LOSS OF A CHILD

25

If I could explain how grief worked, I would.

If there's a better word for sadness, I'd use it.

If I can cover these eyes showing my emotions,

I'd forever hide them away.

The void that is becoming inside me

How I wish there were still those little movements

and how I'd wait for you to explore your little home.

But how I wish I could've met you for a few hours,

even minutes. But I'd also love it if it was a lifetime with my dearest baby.

FEARS

Once again, I'm standing in the bathroom,

Staring and waiting for the little tool

to show me one or two lines.

Heavy breathing, thumping heart,

nail-biting, and toes tapping the floor.

I closed my eyes to catch a moment.

But I'm hoping when I open them again,

there'll be a result to end this agony.

One line.

I looked closely.

Two lines.

There are two lines.

What should I do?

How am I going to take this?

Should I be happy?

I don't know.

I'm not sure.

Because the last time I was on cloud nine,

it got my knees touching the hard and cold ground.

RAINBOW BABY

27

I've been waiting for you, my little one.

I was both happy and concerned.

It became quiet and calm after a while,

but I didn't want to get ahead of myself.

So, I waited.

Thus, when we checked with you,

I had hoped I could turn back time.

Trade and do anything just to do so.

But, the few moments I had with you,

I'm still happy I got the chance to feel you.

It may be in this constricted tummy of mine,

You will always stay in this beating heart of mine.

PART TWO:

POSTPARTUM AND NEWBORN BREASTFEEDING

A MOTHER'S LOVE

In the depths of night, when all is still,

A mother's love, an unbreakable will.

She cradles her child, so gentle and warm,

Protecting them from any harm.

Through sleepless nights and endless cries,

She soothes their fears and wipes their eyes.

With tender touch and whispered words,

She comforts them, their hearts she stirs.

A mother's love, a guiding light,

Through every storm, she holds them tight.

She teaches them to walk and run,

To chase their dreams, to have some fun.

In every milestone, big or small,

She's there to catch them when they fall.

A mother's love, a constant embrace,

A bond that time cannot erase.

THE SMALL BATTLEFIELD

Singing lullabies,

Telling stories

and sometimes wearing them out.

It's a real battlefield.

Where there are soldiers

And their enemies on the other side.

It is aiming for a treaty,

Some form of convincing,

For the sake of the chores and cleaning.

The soldiers should be left sleeping,

Otherwise, there's nothing to get done.

SHOULD I SLEEP, EAT, OR…?

32

Once the baby sleeps,

I hope to get free for a little bit.

But how do I do that

When my body feels heavy,

My eyes are getting drowsy,

and these feet I am now dragging.

Is it beside the baby?

The bed?

The sink?

The stove?

The TV, some shows?

Or the…?

FRAGILE RESILIENCE

33

Everything hurts.

Inches of stitches,

My will power sucked out,

and my voice cracking

now and then.

I know these are negatives,

But I'm trying to look for the positive.

Though it seems my hunt

has already stopped in its track.

Beside me is something fragile

and should be handled with the utmost care.

And I believe this nullifies everything I just said.

MILK

34

Tender breast begins to fill with leaky milk.

It spills out at times,

colostrum ready to nourish you.

Full and engorged,

painful to touch, and achy nipples

but all worth it to help you grow.

LIQUID GOLD

35

He cuddled close.

He felt secure,

his mother's milk was near.

He snuggled up close

with his adorable nose.

His hand touched his food

as the liquid gold touched his tongue.

The smell of his skin

as a mother provided him nourishment.

PUBLIC STARE DOWN

Do not let others judge.

Mama, you know best.

Some will not approve and be critical.

Others will understand.

Just do you.

Listen to your heart.

Let them stare —

a stare down.

Feed your hungry child, here or there,

don't give their eyes any care.

A store?

A restaurant?

At a birthday party?

It's liquid gold.

Nourishment —

bottle or boob, they are one and the same.

THE MAGIC OF A MOTHER'S TOUCH

With a gentle touch, she heals their pain,

A mother's touch, like sunshine after rain.

She kisses their boo-boos, wipes away their tears,

Her touch brings comfort, erases their fears.

In her embrace, they find warmth and peace,

A mother's touch, a love that won't cease.

She holds them close, her touch a balm,

A soothing melody, a healing calm.

Her touch is magic, it has the power,

To mend broken hearts, to make them flower.

A mother's touch, a divine connection,

A bond that's unbreakable, a love without question.

UNBREAKABLE BOND

Forever treasuring this.

The bond we have.

As you nurse, cuddling me close,

Staring back at me, I stare at you.

Moments I am going to miss —

I'll treasure this.

Knowing one day, this bond will end.

New bonds will form,

new ways to comfort you.

Oh, but this bond I will never forget.

As I sit here, staring at you,

it brings a smile to my lips

as I bring comfort to you.

A MOTHER'S VOICE

39

Her voice, a melody, sweet and clear,

Guiding her children, calming their fear.

With every word, she plants a seed,

A mother's voice, the strength they need.

BABY TEETHING

Baby teething,

fangs growing, pain ignited.

It is the birth of new teeth.

Wanting to eat,

but the soreness of the gums

won't allow such a thing.

In tears, crying,

while I'm losing my sanity.

Coming in spurts,

hoping it won't last long.

"Teeth!" I yell.

Please, just poke through.

Lord, take his pain away.

Try singing to him,

massage his gums,

even a teether—

Nothing seems to help.

Oh Lord, please just let them pop!

ME AND I

Mom! Mama! Mother!

Here and there, they call.

After bearing newborns,

my identity has become a range of

wife, mother, chauffeur, nanny, and maid.

No time for myself.

Don't remember who I am,

always a mom, wife,

or something for someone else.

Who am I?

Don't recognize where I went.

I love my duty,

but I miss the old me.

Always busy,

running out of time for myself

but not for the people within this house.

SLEEPLESS NIGHTS

Time to head to bed, they say.

Tuck the kids in—

Dad is already in bed, sound asleep,

and loud snoring coming from the room.

Leftovers are to be put into containers.

Dishes to be put away.

Countertops to be wiped down.

Change into pajamas.

Finally, time to sleep.

Lie down slowly —

the baby starts to cry.

Just the baby and I now.

Baby twisting and turning, starting to fart.

Gesturing for food,

Mommy is there.

Breast out — ready to feed.

Daddy is snoring away.

Next is burping —

spew flew out.

Clothes and diapers changed.

Back to bed, you go.

Mommy's maternal alarm goes off again —

not even two in the morning.

The baby stirred and stared at me,

wanting to eat once more.

Finally —

off to bed, I go.

DROOPY EYES

About sleepy eyes when being a mother

When I close my eyes,

I feel like I'm falling into an abyss.

I often rest my eyes when I sit.

When I'm sure the little ones are asleep

and when they can't stay open anymore.

The caffeine isn't kicking,

So are the energy drinks.

At times like this, there's only one question.

Thus, I stop at my current chore,

When was the last time I hit the bed?

BOOBIES, WHERE DID YOU GO?

45

Sometimes, people ask if they are sisters.

Oftentimes, maybe cousins?

Or perhaps distant relatives?

But for the majority of us girls, women, mothers,

even grandmothers.

They are what we call breasts.

Where the mothers produce milk

and the baby drinks.

Full and aching, but really, it's swollen.

They are breasts that feed and provide.

Though there are times they disappear.

Sizes vary from girl to girl

but one thing you should know,

they are not to be taken lightly

and only used for entertainment.

Whether the cups and numbers are big or small,

they are a part of being a woman.

THE SYMBOL OF PRODUCING

46

Since colors have their respective meaning,

we understand which emotions they express

and tell our eyes.

Since flowers represent each kind of love,

we take note of what and what not

to give to our partners.

Then, pregnancy is the symbol of another human being,

because we anticipate the baby's arrival.

Then, when the baby wails,

we understand they need us by their side.

A MOTHER'S HUG

47

In her embrace, they find solace and peace,

A mother's hug, a love that won't cease.

With arms wide open, she holds them tight,

A hug that comforts, day and night.

PART THREE:
WATCHING THEM GROW — THROUGH THE GOOD, BAD, AND UGLY

TO-DO

In the early morn, with a heart so strong,

A mom's to-do list, oh, how it's long.

From sunrise to sunset, she's on the go,

Juggling tasks, like a pro.

First, she tends to the little ones,

Feeding, dressing, and tying their buns.

With a loving touch and a gentle kiss,

She starts her day with pure bliss.

Next, she tackles the mountain of chores,

Sweeping, mopping, and scrubbing floors.

Laundry piles high, dishes to be done,

She never stops until she's won.

Errands to run, groceries to buy,

She's always on the move, oh my.

Doctor appointments, school events,

She's there for every moment, no pretense.

But amidst the chaos, she finds her peace,

A moment to breathe, to find release.

For in her heart, she knows it's true,

Her to-do list is a labor of love, through and through.

So let's raise a toast to the moms out there,

Whose to-do lists are beyond compare.

Their strength and resilience, a sight to behold,

A testament to a love untold.

TICK TOCK TIME PT. II

The wall clock has already stopped.

Though we are still moving and running.

Its hands have been frozen.

I should be able to find batteries.

Removing the dried-out ones and

Replacing them with fresh-picked ones.

How I wish our time stopped as well

When the clocks around us freeze.

A MOTHER'S WISDOM

53

Her wisdom, a beacon, shining bright,

Guiding her children, with all her might.

With every word, she imparts her truth,

A mother's wisdom, a lifelong pursuit.

CHAOS

The pitter-patter of little feet

coming down the stairs

asking what is for dinner.

Spaghetti, Mac n' cheese; no, wait!

A grilled cheese!

Those moments that steal your heart,

one screaming in pain from teething,

the other just pouts.

Ah, the joys of motherhood —

It is what life is all about.

From late-night tantrums to early-morning grunts,

through all the sickness, scrapes, and bumps.

The kisses, hugs, the "I love you",

The look in their eyes, to their giggles.

Oh, such fond memories.

I would not change it for the world — never.

The laundry piling, and toys left on the floor,

the moments we live for.

From making sure they are fed,

reading a bed story while tucking them in

a lifetime of tears, laughter —

Oh, such fond memories being made

through this journey called

Motherhood — oh, at its finest.

MOM(ENTS) PT. I

I find myself in the field of flowers,

With each petal holding a memory.

I try to look at each one,

Bits of everything I can recall,

and some, totally out of the window now.

But that's okay.

They can be replaced with other great

and sincere memorabilia

of what I have now —

and what I will have soon.

HOT SHOWER

57

It's one of the most favorable things I enjoy.

Standing still for an hour,

Limited movements in place

While the heaviness and wetness of heat

drip down my face and to my feet.

Soothing, oh-so relaxing.

A mini vacation where I can think.

Similar to a forgiving mother's embrace,

A liquid form of sweetest praise.

Oh, such a refreshing hot shower.

STEP MOMS

Being a stepmom is never easy.

Wanting to be a part of the children's lives,

but remember you are not the mom.

But you're their mom.

Their second mom.

You care for and love them just as their own.

Being a stepmom is hard.

Growing up wanted nothing to do with my stepmom.

Now I love her so,

Hoping and praying for this sort of relationship,

one day, maybe one day.

Stepmoms are just as important,

but don't want to overstep,

as I am a mom too.

Don't want to take anyone's place.

It's a parent wanting to give extra love.

Not wanting to replace the MOM.

My daughter has a stepmom,

and for that I'm grateful.

Stepmoms,

you're loved and seen too.

BREAKING HABITS

I don't want to pass down

the trouble I went through

while I was in the process

of learning about the world and myself.

If I need to break bonds and ties,

I'll do so for my babies' future.

They are all that matters

and they are my priority.

Breaking the responses I was accustomed to,

Breaking outdated thoughts and beliefs,

and finally, breaking free from its sources.

I want my little ones to know the good and bad,

the right amount of boundaries, and

the healthy way of viewing the world.

NO TIME TO PASS ME BY

There are so many things I want to say and do.

Crossing them out of my bucket list.

Though I also have the everyday bits

of what I want to accomplish.

I love you.

Can I hug you?

How are you feeling?

Just wanted to say I thought of you today.

Texting to check on you.

Do you want to hang out with me?

I'd love it if you can come to hang out with us.

These questions, phrases, and sentences,

all have a common denominator.

I don't want to miss a chance

when it comes to the people I love.

LAUNDRY, ENDLESS LAUNDRY

A cycle of changing.

When you get out of the shower,

Going out to run some errands,

Hanging out with friends,

Out to brunch and maybe hit the movies.

Every chance we get, we change.

Thus, when you look at that one corner

Inside your house,

Every piece of clothing just stares back.

When do you plan on washing us?

OVERSTIMULATED

I am

overwhelmed,

overworked,

and

overstimulated.

But I want to be

well-rested,

full of sleep,

and

anything with the word

"over."

But I'll accept it if it's over-loved.

MOM(ENTS) PT. II

63

I am a mother;

I am a woman.

I am the light of my family,

as they are to me.

I am able to produce a human in my belly,

and I am able to give birth.

I have dreamt of being a mother,

Now I am one.

HANDBOOK

I am not a fan of reading

But became one during pregnancy.

Curious about the duplicating cells,

Gender checking,

When the belly gets too big

and too hard to carry.

It didn't matter how many books,

I wanted to make sure I'm doing it right.

When my baby finally came,

there wasn't a warning to blame.

No one knew the right thing to do,

only the best option out of all the others.

It is all scary and unfamiliar

but entering this new chapter,

I say it'll be full of learning and love.

They say experience is the best teacher,

then hang on tight to my hand,

Let's go through this together.

Not by the book and words,

But by what life teaches.

THE STRENGTH OF A MOTHER

In the face of adversity, she stands tall,

A warrior, a protector, giving her all.

With strength and grace, she faces each day,

Balancing the chaos that comes her way.

She carries the weight of the world on her shoulders,

Yet her love for her children only grows bolder.

Through sleepless nights and endless chores,

She never complains, her heart always soars.

Her love knows no bounds, it knows no end,

She's a mother, a confidant, a lifelong friend.

She teaches them to be brave and kind,

To never give up, to always find

The beauty in life, the joy in each day,

To cherish the moments, to laugh and play.

A mother's strength, a force to be reckoned,

Her love, her power, forever unbroken.

THE FUTURE OF TOMORROW

"I can't wait for tomorrow, Mom!"

My toddler exclaimed.

Right on time just before closing his eyes.

He always tells me about tomorrow,

Even though he comes home to me

Full of sorrow.

In his eyes, tomorrow is unprecedented

and the start of another blank canvas.

How I wish he'd stay with that view,

No matter how much he'll grow.

Tomorrow is another start,

and I'm beginning to look forward to it

with him.

TO MY MOM

How are you doing?

I hope you are well

as I have prayed you'd be.

Seeing as I am a mother now,

I have always dreamt of how

it is to be like you.

The morning breeze when you wake me up.

When I'd ask "What's for dinner?"

Those nights when I cry my eyes out

because of boys mishandling my heart.

How are you doing now?

I hope and pray you feel me

every time and everywhere you go.

Please do be on the lookout

because you'll be the first one I'd call

whenever and wherever I experience mishaps.

I was once your little one,

and I'd pray to God to be yours again

even in my next lifetime.

THE DANCE OF MOTHERHOOD

In the dance of motherhood, she takes the lead,

Guiding her children with every word and deed.

She twirls and spins, with grace and poise,

Nurturing their dreams, their hopes she employs.

She teaches them to find their own rhythm,

To dance through life, to embrace each prism.

With patience and love, she shows them the way,

To follow their hearts, to never sway.

In the ups and downs, the twists and turns,

She's there to catch them, her love always burns.

The dance of motherhood, a beautiful art,

A symphony of love, a masterpiece from the start.

A MOTHER'S LEGACY

69

In the tapestry of life, she weaves her thread,

Leaving behind a legacy, even after she's dead.

Her love, her wisdom, forever imprinted,

In the hearts of her children, never to be tinted.

She teaches them to be strong and true,

To stand up for what they believe, to pursue

Their dreams with passion, to never give in,

To always strive for greatness, to always win.

Her legacy lives on in every smile,

In every act of kindness, going the extra mile.

A mother's love, a gift that keeps giving,

A legacy that transcends, forever living.

A MOTHER'S SACRIFICE

In the depths of her heart, a sacrifice is made,

A mother's love, an eternal trade.

She gives up her dreams, her desires, her time,

To ensure her children's lives are sublime.

She puts their needs before her own,

Her love for them, forever shown.

Through sleepless nights and weary days,

She never wavers, she never strays.

A mother's sacrifice, a selfless act,

Her love for her children, an unwavering pact.

She gives them wings to soar and fly,

To reach for the stars, to touch the sky.

DIAL TONE

Everyone has their first time.

But there are moments where

I reach for my phone and dial.

The line rings and I wait.

Then, click it goes.

The first voice I heard

when I was a crying baby.

The first words that I said back then,

will always be the first words I'll say

every time you pick up the phone.

"Mom?"

ACKNOWLEDGMENTS

I would like to express my deepest gratitude and appreciation to my husband for his unwavering support and understanding throughout the process of writing Mommyhood at its Finest. Your encouragement and belief in me have been invaluable, and I am truly grateful for your patience during those late nights and weekends spent working on this book. Thank you for always being there to lend a helping hand and for being my biggest cheerleader.

To my incredible kids, you are the driving force behind this book. Your boundless love, endless energy, and unique perspectives on motherhood have inspired me beyond measure. Your laughter, tears, and everyday moments have shaped the stories within these pages. Thank you for being my constant source of inspiration and for reminding me of the joys and challenges of mommyhood every day.

I would also like to extend my heartfelt thanks to Dominique, a fellow author and mother, whose own motherhood books have been a constant source of inspiration for me. Your words have resonated deeply with me, and your stories have provided me with a sense of camaraderie and understanding during the ups and downs of motherhood. Thank you for sharing your experiences and for reminding me that I am not alone on this journey.

Dominique, your dedication to writing about the joys and challenges of motherhood has been a guiding light for me. Your honesty, vulnerability, and unwavering commitment to sharing your story have inspired me to do the same. Thank you for paving the way and for showing me that our stories as mothers are worth telling.

To Dominique, thank you for being a source of inspiration and for reminding me of the power of storytelling. Your books have touched the lives of countless mothers, including mine, and I am grateful for the impact you have made. Your words have given me the courage to share my own experiences and to embrace the beauty and chaos of mommyhood.

I would like to acknowledge God for His guidance and blessings throughout the journey of writing my book, "Mommyhood at its Finest." His divine intervention and grace helped me become a mother, and I am forever grateful for His love and support. Without His presence in my life, this book would not have been possible. Thank you, God, for your unwavering love and for blessing me with the beautiful gift of motherhood.

To my husband, my kids, Dominique, and God, I am eternally grateful for your love, support, and understanding. Without you, this book would not have been possible. Your presence in my life has made me a better writer, a better mother, and a better person. Thank you for being my inspiration and for being a part of this incredible journey.